SOULFLOWERS

AMAL BACKER

ISBN 979-888555526-5

for the lovers, dreamers and believers of all things magical

Contents

Contents

1. inner worlds

home

deep down in the tangled woods that grows in my mind

I've built a home,

away from home, away from the walls of my comfort zones,

hidden away from the king and queens and ways of the past,

invisible to the war crazy lords

and to the gods ofcourse.

In the dark and dangerous woods that grows in my mind,

I've built a home,

a home lacking laws, without highs and lows,

a home for all the mad peaople I've ever known,

but I've been alone for so long

I wish to take you there

and I can take you there,

only if you'd read me to sleep and freedom.

a crack in the sea

I fit in at the middle of the road, as the world pass by, I dust up and disappear, on the walls of my room I roam, when the crowd leaves the scene I crawl to sweet spaces in my head, in a cloud, a crack in the sea am I, dreamy looming nightscapes of a life not lived not a nightmare, not anymore, although I run from me, I belong to not even me.

dance of the wild

This wildness dance

within me.

Rush me

to the skies and crush me

down to my roots.

It grows around me

surrounds me,

shooks me off of the

dead deeds of the past,

drags me to the core

and burns the seeds of tomorrow.

This wildness grows

within me,

I've made it my sanctuary.

little cedars and

floating groves

and spirit birds

do ritual dance with the witches

and it heals me.

My sacrifice is to refrain from normalcy.

pardon me,

I'm no part of nature but Nature is me.

Nature's nature is being wild and free.

You can't define me, cage or contain me.

This dance of the wild do burdens me, darkness clouds me

but in there, in that ominous darkness

there's a trail left by ancients.

I follow it. Blindfolded.

May it lead me to my true nature.

Thus find me not in the obvious lands,

for nature is wild and free,

So are we.

inner worlds

I failed to keep in touch with your worlds.

I've been chasing my paradise lost.

How well are you in touch with your worlds?

Do you still look at the moon?

Or are you busy at nights

fixing up the broken pieces of that beautiful flowervase

that you threw at your father?

Does the scent of night bring you

memories of your beloved?

Does the morning breeze smell of

perished pasts?

Do you regret your pasts?

Is it a fantasy? Your reality.

How do you grasp your reality? Your fantasy.

Is it a dream for you ? This life.

Does your god look like you?

Do you bleed blues?

Is it dark inside you? Does it hurt?

Do they dim their lights for you?

Can you see the roads ahead? The pits ahead.

Does the world make it easy for you?

Or do they make you cry?

Or do you sing instead ? Like you used to

Do you sing when you're scared

and alone in the dark?

Is it all a dream for you? This life.

When you wake up, will you remember me?

Do you know me? Do you Know you?

Do you remember your heart?

Your heart

Is your Art

Do you try not to sell your heart? Is it hard?

Have you lost the parts? Your Art

Which blooms flowers in the yards of the powerless.

Or have the world made you powerless?

Have you lost the parts? Of your heart.

Patch it up.

Your heart Is your Art.

Try not to sell your heart.

Though I'm still fixing up that flowervase,

It's all a dream for me. This life. My reality, a fantasy.

When I wake up,

When we're together yet alone

Still afraid of the dark

Will you sing me that song? And can we not sell our hearts?

Instead Forget the pasts

And share our worlds?

longing to belong

you don't belong to everywhere you fit in

you don't belong to the constant crowds you find yourself in

you are what you are alone,you are your ultimate solitude

you belong to the unknown, you belong to the wilderness within

you are grey, white and dark blues, nature's random changes

you are both summer and spring

nature itself

struggling inside a text book page

just strip away that costume they gave

throw the role and run down the hall

long to belong in the now, in the moment

Be there and just blend in there

be you and be in love

melt within, naked, in truth,

and grow, where you belong.

individuality

Individuality.

The You in You. Ultimately.

Your individuality.

You this marvelous creation of an unknown entity.

You the heart that ache to hug the mother tree.

Fight the good fight. Escape mediocrity.

Hold what you have, a few of these moments in eternity.

Don't dwell in their hopeless world's charity.

Ask for an ounce of clarity. Stand up for your fucking individuality.

Reject the masses and the collective reality.

Let the ways be a little slippery. Rather not give in to their trickery.

Your individuality. Stronger than the storms rushing through a mountain peak.

You be what you seek.

You. Ultimately.

You. How you walk. How you talk. How you water the plants.

Your heart. Your laugh. Your dagger sharp smile. The color in it. The power in it.

The love lust and pain you hide in it. The light in it. Shade of the dusk in it.

Dust of the world and shyness of a bride in it.

Wear it.

Fear never to share it.

Choose you and rejoice in your choice.

Choose you. Not me. Forget what you got from me. Embrace your goddamn individuality.

Be you. Be you.

Choose yourself. Notoriously.

2. journey home

waiting for the light to fall

We're all green fruits plucked out of plants while they were deepening the roots. We're all green fruits plucked out of plants while they were waiting for the light to fall.

whole

A pebble in my shoe, got to let it go,

wrong lane of the road, busy streets ahead,

put it aside now we'll walk a mile or two,

pretty freaky dark, rain clouds bark,

crowd as crows, cross when they all cross,

a pebble in my shoe, got to let it go,

kneel down, catch it, throw it and move on,

can't stop now we'll see what we can do,

there's nothing else to do lose it, walk easy peasy, go

A thorn in my heavy heart,a secret trapped inside my gut, it just wants out

pretty much deep go tell mom, before it hurts more

father won't know

baby, secret's out now

I feel like I'm home

but the hole is still a hole

and I know only I can make me whole

life, earth

Fall back to Life.
Fall into the spiral neverending,
that is Life.

It's a painful place.
Are you not tired?

There's a call from the mother.
Are you not going?

Let's fall back to us.
Back to her sacred laps.

They've given us names.
But calls us lost.
It's a horrible place.

Life, Earth

Fall back to me.
Lose all the dreams,
They're pulling you up.

Fall through the skies
Let's go back to us.

departure

On an evening at the end of may, I laid lonely by the balcony, looking up the sky. Three birds flew by, a little high, a little more high, still caught my eye, I too wanted to fly, but I didn't fly, not that I couldn't fly, just that I'm a little shy. I was intrigued by their pace, the places they could set gaze, the clouds of dreams they could chase, do they love that they can fly? or do they seek and weep to run and hide? The dusk is not near and a pain needs cure, a breath of the fresh night's air, a picture of what's going on here, afterall a loving whisper from my dear. Another flock of birds appeared, nearer than previous, the dusk is near, they made it clear, your new dawn is but a departure away.

journey home

journey home July ally skies.
To a purple place.
Holding arms. You and I.
To a purple place.
Journey through broke alleys late.
Leaving home. Holding hopes.
Cry now, cry then, try one more time.
Journey home you hopeless boy
Through country roads, be someone's hope.
Journey home. new town old soul.
Kiss the sick ones bye.
Journey home. Baby girl go far.
Through misty snowy,
sweaty muddy lands. Go so far.
Journey home dear. Hope home's not far.

courage to love

It's your own mind that crushes you

The unsatisfactory nerves inside you,

that punishes you.

Billion body cells and atoms that

senses a bad omen, still life inhales you.

It takes courage to spread your love around.

It takes courage to love yourself,

Despite the ups and downs.

It takes courage to forgive.

It takes courage to love again.

Being brave enough to carry on,

For the little things you keep believing on.

3. soulflowers

ephemeral sunshine

We're moving across a pathway of unspoken words suspended between parallel worlds.

I knew not, how to talk to you

I chose the hard accent the heart's accent.

Silence and smiles, and spoke to you in the moon ocean way.

High tides and low tides, mind famished of desire.

Changing you, without changing you,

Ephemeral, yet eternal.

I knew not to talk to you

I chose the mountain sunrise way,

And spoke to you without changing you

but shining on you fleetingly. everyday, eternal.

I let me not, utter a word. afraid.

For words ruin things,

and even a pebble picked up, alters the nature, good or bad, a flood for the fish world.

I let me not utter a word for I intend to love you untouched , unchanged.

I intend to love you each day as sunlight shines through the clouds.

Without changing me, without changing you

as sunlight shines through the clouds.

And I picture us often under an ocean

naked

wearing colors of the nature, partially merging,

sinking in eachother

Pale blue waters and orange sunshine

blending , transcending

drinking desires from the depths of eachother.

Speaking. Laughing

in the Heart's accent. the hard accent.

Ephemeral. Yet Eternal.

theory of our evolution

At the times when times haven't found to be

My Soul seeked a place to bide

Roamed through the woods and got lost in your mist

Love breezed through the valleys and made me blind

Stood still. Became a tree.

Tall and tall and thought I was free.

Spread the branches high

You came in patches of the shades and as rain and storms

Then left me lone in the draughts and fires

and summers of loneliness struck me as thunders at eventide.

You were my sky, every clouds and stars.

I bowed to thee

Weeped and weeped and asked the gods to make me the moon. In you, my sky.

Then times came when times were just found to be

Decades and centuries and infinities came to be

Alone I died and born again and again

As the same tree

Longed to be free

Longed to be the moon in you, my sky.

Longed to die, to be born again, by your side,

As your ocean tides.

You were my sky.

And seas and in all seasons, I weeped again.

But the gods couldn't see, my love for thee

Tears flooded,

became a river

As Decades and centuries and infinities passed by

Tears dried and I began to die.

Rivers dried and became clouds in the sky.

The heavens turned to clouds and You began to rain

Tired old root rotten tree was I And I waited to die.

Years ahead when the heavens cleared my tears you rained,

I opened my heart but began to fall...

You were there all along, and I couldn't see my love.

I had to die and fall into your laps to find you close.

When the times comes when times cease to be

We'll be together again, you whispered to me.

And I still stare at the sky and long to be near you.

Weep and weep and ask the gods to cease the times.

a poem at your feet

I write for you a tender kiss from my heart

I pour my love for you through my lips,

I bow down and recite a poem at your feet

And surrender to you my poetry that's you.

silences

In the silences between my own words,

I sleep and dream of a world we never known.

And in there I'm nothing pretty but your

poetry poetry poetry.

soulflowers

Street to street beat to beat we journey through light to life as to realise we come from far away far, from more more beautiful worlds, So big the magic in you love you come from realms of real rare true vivid colours that bloom soulflowers, verse to verse lows to highs so bright we move we meet along the multiverse of electric waves that bloom soulflowers. In the darkness of a night that refuse to sleep, our intergalactic moon lit minds collide between the light years that you and I we traveled through to shower neon rivers that bloom soulflowers. In the home of lovers we'll be a cloud of mirrors reflecting selfless skies carried by a wind that hums poems that bloom soulflowers.

9 798885 555265

Printed by Libri Plureos GmbH in Hamburg,
Germany